Laguna BEACH

GRAYSCALE COLORING BOOKS

VOLUME 4.

COLOR TEST PAGE

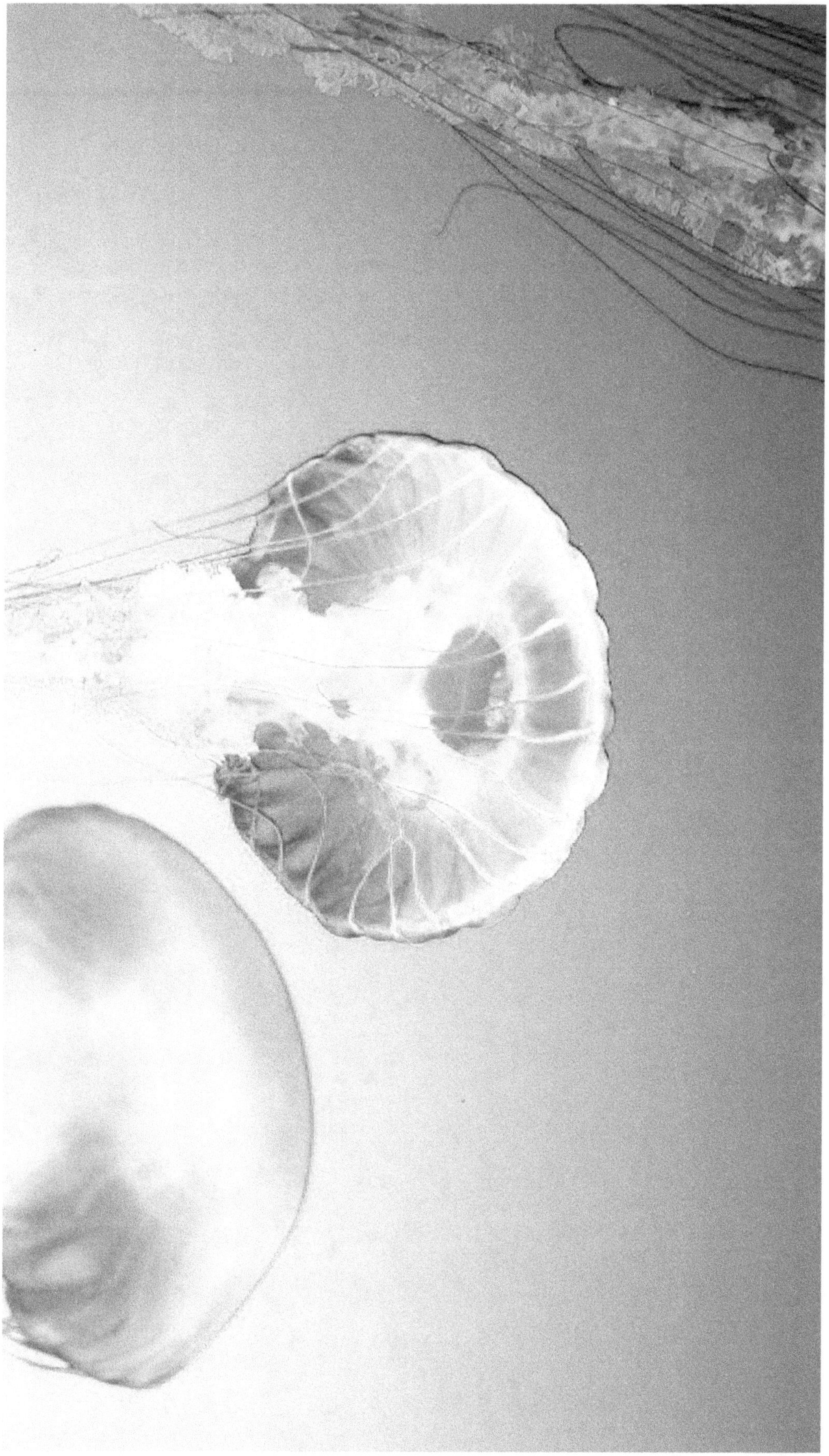

PPB 074
SASIKET
Knack out Bar
phi phi island

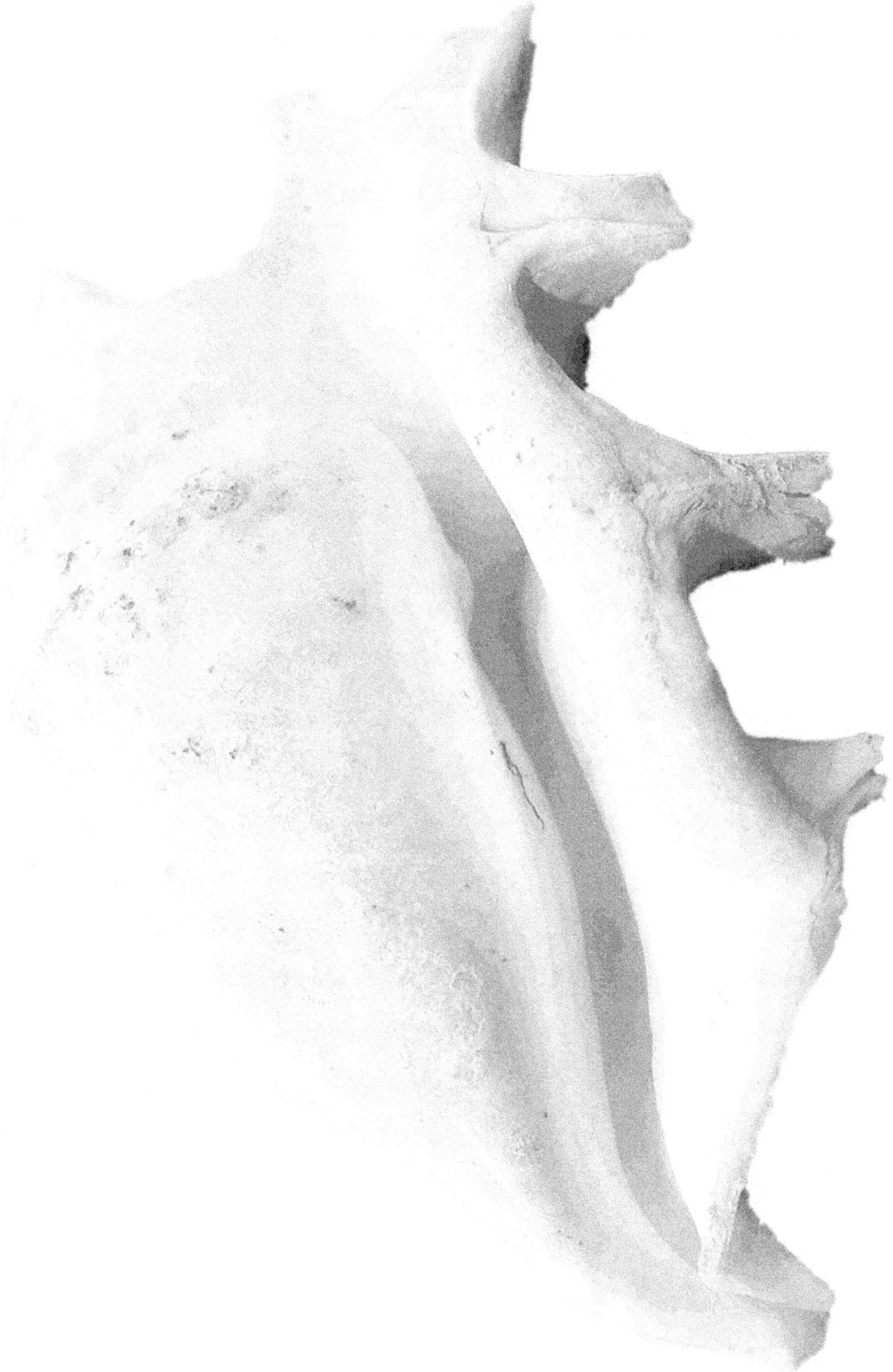

www.ingramcontent.com/pod-product-compliance
Lightning Source LLC
Chambersburg PA
CBHW080558190526
45169CB00007B/2811
9781535228336